Choose Fun

LIVE ON PURPOSE

Toneta Witte

TRILOGY CHRISTIAN PUBLISHERS
TUSTIN, CA

Trilogy Christian Publishers

A Wholly Owned Subsidiary of Trinity Broadcasting Network

2442 Michelle Drive

Tustin, CA 92780

For information, address Trilogy Christian Publishing

Rights Department, 2442 Michelle Drive, Tustin, Ca 92780.

Trilogy Christian Publishing/ TBN and colophon are trademarks of Trinity Broadcasting Network.

For information about special discounts for bulk purchases, please contact Trilogy Christian Publishing.

Manufactured in the United States of America

Trilogy Disclaimer: The views and content expressed in this book are those of the author and may not necessarily reflect the views and doctrine of Trilogy Christian Publishing or the Trinity Broadcasting Network.

10 9 8 7 6 5 4 3 2 1

Library of Congress Cataloging-in-Publication Data is available.

ISBN 978-1-64773-460-2

ISBN 978-1-64773-461-9 (ebook)

Contents

Acknowledgement

I want to thank my family for always supporting me, and for allowing me to share some of our private moments in life together and our experiences, both good and not so good. I am so proud of every single one of them and blessed to be a part of this loving and God-serving family.

A special Thank you, to my youngest daughter Alyssa for assisting me in the final editing process.

All my love!

Choose Fun!

It all began on a road trip to California from Texas. Our family was originally from California, but one by one we all began moving to Texas. I am Toni, a mother of four—three daughters, Annette, Regina, and Alyssa; and one son, Richie. Well, my second daughter Regina was having her first child's baby shower in California. So, my oldest daughter and I and her four children: Ellie, fourteen years old, Joey, thirteen, Jacob, eight, and Andrew, six, all got in the Expedition and drove out to California for the shower. Which, by the way, was fantastic! While we were there, we decided to go to Disneyland. So much fun! But when you have teenagers, you never know which way it will go. Well, Joey decided that he did not want to go to Disneyland with the family, but of course his mom said, "We are all going!" Joey didn't just have an opinion that he didn't want to go; he was adamant, so he was grouchy and in a bad mood, and angry that he had to go. Well, it was affecting all of us and draining out all the fun. So Annette, his mom, took him aside and said, "You might as well choose fun, because this is going to happen, and you will not ruin it for everyone else!" Joey got the message, and things began to turn around. We all had a great time, as it turned out. I'm not sure Joey ever really loved the day, but we did not hear about it either way.

As we left California, we decided to stop at as many tourist attractions as we could find. Our motto for the whole trip was, "Choose Fun." With four children in a car for an extended amount of time, someone was always giving their opinion. We saw the tallest thermometer, we spent the night in Las Vegas and saw the beautiful lights, and we had dinner at Planet Hollywood.

We all had a really great time! Now it was on to Hoover Dam! As you drive into the view of the magnificent Hoover Dam there are signs that read, "Turn your radio to [a specific station] and you will get all the 'dam' information." Before I go on, I must explain that there is no profanity in our vocabulary—really, we just don't use it. It's a real testimony to my husband; his "angry" words were *knucklehead* and *dip-stick*. His reputation was amazing, even to people who worked with him.

We had a trucking business and profanity was rampant, but Ron, my husband, never took part, and everyone knew it. One time a disgruntled employee was talking badly about Ron, trying to start trouble, so he told the other drivers a made-up story about how Ron had cursed him out. Well, everyone knew he was lying, because they knew Ron and he wasn't like that! So, our family just doesn't speak those words. Back to our trip: when we turned the radio to the "dam" station, it was a man's voice, very monotone. He said, "If you would like to see the 'dam' tour, you may go to the 'dam' gift shop and take the 'dam' elevator down." Well, that was all it took—the kids thought it was hilarious and began asking to go to the "dam" gift shop, to see the "dam" tour, and saying that the "dam" view was amazing! We all laughed until we cried. Everything you could say about the "dam" was funny. After we left the "dam" area and got back on the road, we said, "Okay, no more 'dam' jokes." We all agreed, but along the drive someone would come up with, "I sure liked that 'dam' view," and we would all start laughing again! It was fun, and we still laugh about it today. Now on our way, we stopped at the Cadillac Ranch and wrote on the cars—everyone liked that. Now almost home, we decided our last stop would be the "Big Texan," a steakhouse with a big cowboy in front, definitely a tourist stop. Well, now Ellie decided that she'd had enough road trip, and said, "We're almost home; let's just keep driving." Of course we said, "You might as well 'Choose Fun,' because this is going to happen!" By now, everyone knew that choosing a good attitude was better for everyone. We had a great and memorable road trip! Since the trip, after we all got home, the term "Choose Fun" has come up many times, and now the kids are grown and realize that "Choosing Fun" is a way of life!

Our pastor used to say that a one-word definition of *life* is "choices." So true—we have so many each day. If we choose to have a good attitude, to give people the benefit of the doubt, to smile, to be the light and joy in situations, we can absolutely help others to "Choose Fun." Our attitude impacts others; we can help bring people down or lift them up! We can bring hope in desperate times and grace in sad times. There is always room for redemption and forgiveness!

Ellie is twenty-six years old now and married to a wonderful man, Cody. They have three beautiful children and are amazing parents.

Joey is twenty-five years old, also married, to a great girl, Ginny. They are youth leaders at their church.

Jacob and Andrew are involved in their youth group, music, and sports. They are all serving God with all their hearts, and I am so proud of them!

Choose a better life and "Choose Fun."

REFLECTION: CHOOSE FUN!

This message is really about our attitude in life. We can choose to be angry and upset—letting our emotions give us a bad attitude, causing us to lose our joy—and to sit and stew in our desires, having a pity party because we didn't get to do exactly what we wanted in that moment.

The fact is that everything we say—and the way we act—affects the people around us.

With this behavior we can actually suck the fun out of a room or an event that could have been a great time for everyone.

1. Have you ever been somewhere when this happened—maybe a couple quarrelling at dinner in your presence? It is very uncomfortable and definitely brings a different atmosphere to the night.

2. Have you ever had this happen to you? Take a minute and reflect on maybe a temper flare-up or just a bad attitude, because someone else made all the decisions you wanted to make without even asking you.

3. Check your attitude when you are challenged to have to do something you really do not want to do, but everyone else does!

What does the Word say?

Philippians 2:3-5 (KJV) "Let nothing be done through strife or vainglory; but in lowliness of mind let each esteem others better than themselves. Look not every man on his own things, but every man also on the things of others. Let this mind be in you, which was also in Christ Jesus."

Proverbs 17:22 (KJV) "A merry heart doeth good like a medicine: but a broken spirit drieth the bones."

Galatians 5:22,23 (KJV) "But the fruit of the Spirit is love, joy, peace, longsuffering, gentleness, goodness, faith, meekness, temperance: against such there is no law."

Galatians 6:9 (KJV) "And let us not be weary in well doing: for in due season we shall reap, if we faint not."

Remember, we have the ability to make a choice to change our attitude and to make a better decision—to sacrifice our own desires for the good of others. It's the way of the Gospel, the integrity of living a "love life." This life is what draws others to the Good News of the grace of Jesus Christ.

God is faithful and will give us the desires of our hearts in due season. The more we do for others above ourselves, the more blessings are bestowed on us.

Life is Short

When you're young a year seems like such a long time, but as you get older five years can seem like the blink of an eye. Each day is so precious. The Bible, in its wisdom, tells us to live in today, for we don't know what tomorrow brings. Today is all we have, for sure and for now, so make it worth living. If we all lived as if today is all there is, how many decisions would we change? Take time to enjoy each other and even the beauty that God has given us to partake of. I usually walk every day, and one day as I was walking my usual path, it came to me how beautiful the hillside was, and it was like all the colors came alive. But the color was green—as I looked, it was as if God was showing me His splendor and design with just the color green. There were deep green leaves and light green moss, and grass that was dewy and bright and fresh. It's really hard to explain, but the colors of all the greens were amazing! I began to realize that God is so good to us that He didn't just give us color, but the magnificence and abundance of just one color is for us to enjoy. His love and care for us is everlasting, beautiful, and wonderful to us all, if we only take a minute to see it. In Jeremiah 29:11 (NIV) it says, "I know the plans I have for you... plans to give you hope and a future." And in Jeremiah 33:3 (NIV), "Call to me and I will answer you." It's really easy to say "have a good attitude," or "change your outlook," but in times of sorrow and hardships we must keep our eyes on Jesus. He never leaves us or forsakes us, even in our darkest moments. Call on Him and give Him a chance to help you and comfort you.

One day I came home from work, and my husband Ron and my son Rich were finishing a courtyard patio in the front yard of our home. My daughter Annette stopped by to see the finished product also. They showed us their work and were so proud of it and excited to see our faces and reactions! Of course, we loved it! As we were admiring it, some friends stopped by on their motorcycles; they were all going to get some parts at the Harley Davidson motorcycle shop. Ron and Rich were also going. I stayed home to make dinner, and Annette went home to make dinner for her family. It was about twenty minutes later that my phone rang; it was my son Rich. He told me that my daughter was coming back to get me to go to the hospital. There had been an accident with Ron. I had no idea what had happened.

My daughter came, and we went to the hospital. All the riding friends were there, and my son was pacing. I guess I was just oblivious, because I was sure it was just a minor accident and he would be fine. (We've always ridden dirt bikes and dune buggies, so a minor mishap wasn't unheard of.) I went in and asked to see my husband, but they led me into a room full of the people they had ridden with. I didn't understand and started getting angry that I still hadn't seen my husband and had not been told anything! I told the nurse, "I need to see my husband right now!" At that point she said she was sorry, but he was gone. I still did not understand and was getting very angry with her. Finally, she said, "Ma'am, he's gone." I did not believe her; I said, "I need to see him! Now!" So, she led me back to him. He had been hit by an SUV and was dead on impact. My son was there and had tried to revive him, but of course he could not. I stayed in that room for hours, until they made me leave because the mortuary was there to take him. My son and daughters and sons-in-law were there also; we were all in disbelief. It was so sudden and unexpected, it did not seem real. We all went to Annette's house and stayed together for a week. My youngest daughter and her husband flew in from California that night. We hardly spoke. The realization that Ron was gone—and that we would never speak to him again, or hold him, or tell him we loved him—was beginning to sink in. Our hearts were broken! While trying to make funeral arrangements and take care of life's ongoing needs, we realized that life as we knew it was gone! One thing we took from that day is that life is fleeting, time is valuable, and no one knows the day or time of their death. Love each other now. Forgive, embrace, appreciate, and cherish each other, for this might be your last encounter together this side of heaven.

I was seventeen when I married Ron; we were so happy, and he loved God with all his heart and his children just as much! It is a great loss, but we know we shall be reunited in heaven someday.

In Psalm chapter 23, verse 4 (KJV) it says, "Yea, though I walk through the valley of the shadow of death, I will fear no evil: for thou art with me; thy rod and thy staff they comfort me." The rod and staff represent the love of a shepherd for the sheep, to keep them in a safe place—not letting them get lost or hurt. Jesus does that for us. When my husband passed away to be with Jesus, I read this scripture, and it became so real to me. I saw it in a different way, even though I had read it many times. I knew now as I walked through the valley of the shadow of my husband's death that I would make it. Ron and I were so in love, even after all the years together. We were best friends; he took great care of me and loved me completely.

I was afraid that I could not live without him, nor did I really want to. God never let me go, and He showed me His Word in a new light. His rod and His staff, they comforted me. He makes me lie down in green pastures and leads me to the still waters; my cup runneth over. Surely goodness and mercy shall follow me all the days of my life.

God is good. I go to Him for everything, and I mean everything—even if I need a parking space in a crowded mall, I call on Him and say, "Oh, Lord, please let me find one close." I can honestly say that ninety percent of the time, I have found a great parking spot. Seems trivial, I know, but that is how much I know He cares for me. His Word says He knows the number of hairs on our heads. So, He knows your deepest thoughts and hurts and sorrows. The Bible says that to everything there is a season, a time, and a purpose under the heavens. Don't be discouraged through times of hardship; this too will pass. It says He has made everything beautiful in its time. Ask, and you will receive; knock, and the door will be opened to you. God is a gentleman and will not push Himself on you. Call on Him—He's there waiting for the moment you let Him in. The Lord is good; His mercy endures forever!

I now have sixteen grandchildren and three great-grandchildren, and even though we have all had hard times—two precious stillborn baby boys, Isaac and Levi, and several miscarriages for my daughters—God is still just and faithful to keep us in His arms of love, and to bring us through the shadow of death and hardships. The heritage of love of God and faith is truly alive in my family, because my husband and I set a standard; God is faithful to keep that which we've committed to Him. God is truly good all the time! I still wish I had told my husband more how much I appreciated him and how great a provider he was, and that I loved how he loved me. But those days are gone. So, don't be regretful. Remember, yesterday is gone, and tomorrow may never come; today is all we really have for sure, so say it while you can!

One day I was in Walmart getting a battery for a watch I had. The girl behind the counter tried to get the battery out, but the top would not let it loose—she tried all the tools and none would budge it. In my mind I was thinking, *Oh, Jesus, please let it get loose.* I knew that I should say it out loud, but something held me back. I left without a new battery, but worse, I didn't listen to the Holy Spirit and say those words. I honestly think God would have let it get loose and shown the woman the power of the name of Jesus. I was so sorry; I repented, and even though I know He forgave me, I was regretful for a long time. I never saw the woman again, even though I often shopped there. Now, if the Lord gives me a word, I say it. The regret of that day has stayed with me, and I don't want to let my Lord down again. Lord, help me to be in Your love and in Your service, so that others will see Your love and greatness. After that, I was more sensitive to the Lord. I began praying for a group of people, four men and one woman. I woke up one night, with God impressing on me to go to them and tell them, "Jesus wants you to know He loves you." I always saw them in the late afternoon as I would walk my dog, and they would be sitting at a table at the park. This day, I walked up and said hello; they asked me to sit, so we sat and chatted. They told me that they come every summer from India to see their grandchildren and help take care of them, and then go back to India in the fall. Because their names were difficult to say, I gave them nicknames; they laughed and were very friendly. Before I left, I told them that in my sleep Jesus told me to let them know that He loves them. First there was silence, then one man began to tell me of many very good and important men of their faith. He asked if I had heard of them, and I said yes, that Hari Krishna was very well known in California, where I was from. And yes, there are a lot of great men; but there is only one Jesus. They got a little quiet, but seemed to be pondering what I had said. I repeated that He loved them and was the way to God. They often asked me back to their table and we talked of life in India. One day a new man came; he seemed to be a personality that overtook their conversation, so when I came by and said hello, he asked me, "Why do you speak to us?" I said, "Why not?" He laughed and asked me to sit, and he told me I was the first white person to talk to him. I did not get much said in the conversation that night. We all said goodbye, for they would soon be leaving to go back to India. I really enjoyed our time together, and I still pray for them all.

"Choosing Fun" is not just about having fun, or even having a good attitude, but it is much more a frame of mind to serve God on purpose. It is not letting circumstances predict your happiness or lack thereof, but living on a higher plane. Serving God in all we do. Thanking Him for things we don't understand or like. The Bible tells us to give thanks at all times. Our mind doesn't understand that, but our spirit needs it. He is the lamp to my feet and the light to my path. Trust is so essential to a spiritual and physical walk with Christ. It's what brings us to the peace that passes all understanding. When I read of Stephen, the follower of Jesus who was stoned for telling the truth of who Jesus was, I see that he was not afraid, and the Bible says his face shone like an angel. He cried out to God to not hold this offense against them. He forgave them, even to death (Acts 6:5).

It's been over eleven years now since Ron went to be with Jesus. I still don't understand why, but I know in whom I believe! I can tell you: God took us all through that heartache, loss, and sorrow, and we all serve Him with all our hearts. We trust Him with our lives and our children, no matter what. But it's a "new trust" that through that valley of the shadow of death, He never leaves us or forsakes us!

So here is the lesson: Love each other every day. Lay down offenses and hurts, and forgive. With God, all things are possible. You may only have today; make it great!

REFLECTION:
LIFE IS SHORT

We sometimes take our lives for granted. It's easy to do—we make our plans and fix our calendars accordingly. Every day seems to run into another, and before we know it, it's a week or even a month later. Where does the time go?

With today's technology we can get updates by the minute: the weather, news flashes, and even what's going on with our neighbors on social media. It's a fast-paced world.

1. Stop. Take inventory of what is really important. Rearrange your priorities.
2. Ask and seek God to help you with wisdom to live each day to its fullest.
3. We will all go through loss—maybe a loved one, or a job, or even our own human abilities. Let God bring peace and healing to you today. He is willing and well able to comfort, heal, and restore anything we have come against or are battling.

Ecclesiastes 3:1-4 (KJV) "To everything there is a season, and a time to every purpose under the heaven: a time to be born, and a time to die; a time to plant, and a time to pluck up that which is planted; a time to kill, and a time to heal; a time to break down, and a time to build up; a time to weep, and a time to laugh; a time to mourn, and a time to dance."

Continue reading Ecclesiastes 5-9.

From this, we know that our days are numbered. Everyone has the same amount of time each day: twenty-four hours. So, take thought of what you are doing with your time. Ask God to reveal to you what you need to do or change in your daily schedule to accomplish what God has for you to do!

John 3:16 (KJV) "For God so loved the world, that He gave his only begotten Son, that whosoever believeth in Him should not perish, but have everlasting life."

Be sure that you have asked Jesus into your heart and life. Seek Him for guidance and forgiveness. From this moment on, He will never leave you or forsake you!

Live on Purpose

Choose to make today a better day. When you act, think, and talk positively, it helps others to change their outlook too. Last year there were a lot of changes at work. No one really likes change too much, so already we were a little skeptical about the whole situation. I am a substitute school bus driver for a school district here in Texas. This means that I drive each and any route if someone is out on a given day. Because I am a forty-hour employee, I also work in the office if needed. This year, all office staff was brought over from our other district site. Many changes took place. We used to have an open-door policy to the office, and we could chat and get our own keys. Now it was closed-door, and through the window we were handed our keys. Because basically every piece of paper in the school district now came through this office, physicals, training, and accidents, etc., were to be put into the computer and filed. All very important work, to be done by one woman, Susan. In our break room we were now told to keep the noise down, and occasionally they would come and shut our door. Everyone began to think that Susan was too serious, grouchy, and thought too highly of herself.

Since I had the chance to work in the office and see the inner workings, and the huge work load that Susan was responsible for, I saw that she was none of those things. One day I was in the break room with the other drivers having coffee, and the conversation was about all the changes we'd had. I began to tell them how much I liked Susan and how huge her workload was. That I felt it wasn't fair for her to not have her own office where she could have privacy and be able to concentrate, especially considering all the responsibility that she had. As time went on, and we all got to know Susan and the others in the office better, opinions began to change, and now everyone really appreciates all the work Susan and the others do. Over the summer, walls were put up and Susan finally got her office, and it's much better. My point is: Instead of jumping into conversations and being negative, you can give a positive word and help people to see things in a different way—sometimes even to change their minds and opinions. God wants us to be the light and salt, to bring the good flavor of life to others, showing His love.

Another time some of us drivers were out on a field trip—this one was a trip to a football game. We transport the band kids and stay until the game is over, then return them to the school, usually over about six hours. This is a great time to get to know the other drivers. As we were sitting and talking, one of the drivers, Tim, said he had put in a request for a day off and was denied. All requests were now routed to a new girl in our office, Lori. He was very upset and took it personally, as it was for his daughter's college visit.

Tim had always been very conscientious about taking days off, and he never abused it. He felt it wasn't fair. Well, being his friend, I was upset for him. I said it wasn't right. "Maybe you should go above her; she has no reason to not let you off." I was fueling the fire, as they say. There were other drivers there too. After I got home that night, the Lord really began to deal with me about my attitude. I knew that I had to rectify it. So, I wrote a text in the middle of the night to everyone who was there for the conversation. I said that I was sorry for being so negative, and that I was sure that Lori had no idea how important it was to Tim to take that day off. I said that it was really not my place to stir up the conversation. I apologized to everyone. I received several responses the next morning; one said, "We all do things like that; forget about it." Another said, "Forgiven," and one said, "Don't know what you're talking about." I was so relieved to do what I knew was right—it really set me free. I know it made a difference to others also. We must realize that our words are so important—we can bring peace, joy, understanding, and even a benefit of the doubt to others. The Bible says that we have the power of life and death in our tongue; we must make better choices with what we say. As God's children, every idle word will be judged. I want a clear conscience and to bring joy and life, not despair, to others' lives. This is what God expects of us as His children. I try to get up every day asking God for wisdom and direction to be a source of light and an example of the happiness and peace that we are so freely given. His promises are: the joy of the Lord is my strength; with Christ I can do all things; a merry heart is like a medicine, but a broken spirit dries the bones. The Lord said that He came to mend the brokenhearted. We are a part of that mending by using words of love and encouragement and compassion, with the truth of God's Word.

Another time on a field trip, an incident occurred when the man driving the lead bus, Jerry, was on the radio giving directions to the busses behind to get to our destination together. There were usually five to ten busses, and they wanted us to arrive together. So, the lead driver would usually make sure that everyone had the same route. Well, as we drove on, Jerry got on the radio and asked how everyone was doing in traffic. The last driver in the convoy said, "Don't worry, I know my way; I'll just meet you there."

After we arrived and got off of our busses, Jerry was very angry. He felt she had made a fool of him and took her own route on purpose. He took it very personally; he felt that she made him look like he didn't know what he was doing. Mona, the other driver, had no idea he was so upset.

He was so upset that he called her supervisor, who also was a very good friend of Mona's. The supervisor assured him that she would talk to Mona on Monday. Jerry was sure that the supervisor called her, as it wasn't five minutes later that Mona came over and said, "I'm sorry, Jerry. I was just trying to get here; I meant no harm." Jerry did not accept the apology; he thought she was just trying to cover herself. As the night went on, Jerry was very upset. I began to tell him, "I'm sure it was not personal, and I really don't think she meant any harm. Please let it go; it will make you sick to hold on to anger." It went on for hours. But before the night was over, Jerry went over to talk to Mona, and they worked it all out. I told him that I was very proud of him, and you could see that he felt much better. Later, he said jokingly that I made him do it, but we both know it was his decision—and he was happier for making it!

How quickly we can take offense. After all, we didn't deserve it, or it wasn't our fault. There is always a reason to take offense, but oh, the web we weave, even for ourselves, when we don't forgive and let go of things that can literally rule our lives. Forgiveness is freeing!

It frees us to be happy and feel good. Don't hold on to offenses; they only hurt you in the long run!

One day I was asked to help out in the office at work. Susan gave me a binder full of papers that needed to be shredded, with specific instructions that certain pages were to be left in the binder. It was an easy task, so there I went, shredding away. A friend came up to chat and ask my advice about something. Of course, with my dedication to both work and friend, I continued to shred and chat. At this point you can guess what happened—I shredded papers that were specifically supposed to be left in the binder. I panicked! OMG, did I really do this? Yes, I did. I could act like it didn't happen, or I could go in and confess my faults. I felt so stupid and embarrassed. It was a simple job, and I messed up! I told Susan straight out what I did. I told her how sorry I was. I expected her to be angry. Instead she said, "Okay, what did you shred?" I showed her the binder and she calmly looked at me and said, "Well, that is why I always make copies." I was so relieved and told her how silly I felt and that I was so thankful she had made copies.

I was ready to take my medicine, to be reprimanded and told how important those papers were. But it went another way. Now we joke about my "shredding abilities." Now, when I ask her if there is any shredding to be done, we both get a good laugh out of it.

Sometimes things don't go as we plan. We think we are so up to the task, but life happens and all of a sudden, we feel so inadequate! But the sun will come up tomorrow, and tomorrow is another day! Sometimes we have to laugh at ourselves and put down our pride. We are all human, and all of us make mistakes. Because of that, we learn to be considerate and merciful to others when they make mistakes too. I was so glad that I immediately went and told the truth. I feel like it set a standard of integrity, even when things go wrong. Love always covers a multitude of sins and mistakes. Thank you, Jesus.

REFLECTION: LIVE ON PURPOSE

This chapter is a real-life reflection of things in everyday life. When we are in conversations with others, we can be the influence for a positive or a negative response. It seems today that most people want to talk about everything that is going wrong, or if they're having a bad day. Even in the morning at work, if you ask someone how they are doing they might say, "Well, I'm here."

I will usually follow with, "So glad you are." It usually brings a smile to their face.

We are created to live in God's purpose! What I mean by that is that when we give our hearts to Jesus, we have decided to follow Him. His Word becomes our direction in life. The more we study the Bible (the Word of God), the more we know what God's plan is for us.

John 15:4-5 (KJV) "Abide in me, and I in you. As the branch cannot bear fruit of itself, except it abide in the vine; no more can ye, except ye abide in me. I am the vine, ye are the branches: he that abideth in me, and I in him, the same bringeth forth much fruit: for without me ye can do nothing."

Definition of *purpose*: the reason for which anything is done, created, or exists; a fixed design for a fixed intention.

I believe we have what I call "appointments" in life. If we live on purpose or by design, we can achieve our goals and make a difference in leading others by the testimony of our witness and the fruit of our labor. Be the person who is patient in a long line. Have a smile on your face to share with someone. God will put us in situations where we know we need to say a word of encouragement or help if someone is struggling. Let people know that Jesus loves them right where they are, by the way we show God's love for them.

1. Be ready to be used of God. He wants willing people to be His hands and feet.
2. Every morning, before you start your day, ask the Lord to open your eyes to what He has for you to accomplish this day.
3. We are the light in a dark world; let your light of the love of Jesus shine.

God Knows

God knows you better than you know yourself.

He sees our hearts—the reasons we do things, the reasons we say the things we say, the brokenness, the hurts, the scars of the past. He truly knows you. In Jeremiah 1:5 (NIV) it tells us, "Before I formed you in the womb I knew you, before you were born I set you apart." God has a better way for you. There is power in the name of Jesus! Just saying His name is powerful and can change everything. He brings a real peace to any situation. It is a name of authority, and when you ask Jesus to be Lord of your life, and believe that He is the Son of God, you have the permission to use the name of Jesus to lead others to Christ and to pray for the sick to be healed! God's name is YHWH (Yahweh), meaning I AM. What do you need today? He's our Provider, the Healer of our body, the Savior of our soul, our Shepherd who watches over us and leads us to a better life. He is Shalom, which is our peace. No matter what you've done or what you've been through, God knows.

I grew up in a very unstable home. My father—actually he was my step-dad, but the only father I knew—was angry, verbally abusive, and unpredictable. We lived in chaos and a state of fear, not knowing what mood he might be in on any given night. My mother loved us all very much but was submissive to my dad, and though there were some good times, there were many fights. My mother knew of affairs my dad had over the years, but she always forgave him. Sometimes during conflicts, or if dad came in yelling, my siblings and I would hide in the closet until things calmed down. We had a hallway going between our bedrooms, and lots of nights I felt like I heard footsteps walking. It was scary, and I would hide under my blanket and sometimes wet my bed, too afraid to get up.

When I was eleven years old a lady friend of my mother's told her about Jesus, and we began going to a Pentecostal church. Wow, it was amazing! The woman was a precious older woman who loved God with all her heart. My mother was invited to a Bible study, a ladies' group. I begged to go along, and there I was touched by the Lord. After that I had a burning desire to read the Bible. I began reading from front to back. I learned so much about God and His love, and Jesus, His Son. I asked Jesus to be my Savior, and He did. Things at home were very much the same, but there was a different atmosphere. My mother became bold in Christ and told my dad that things were going to change. One day mom and dad were fighting, and when Dad raised his hand to her, she yelled out, "Jesus!" He went flying across the room! I was amazed! Life did begin to change for the better, little by little. My mother would get up early every morning to pray and read the Bible. I still heard footsteps at night, but now I knew that it was Jesus protecting us. The fear was gone. Oh, how good is God? Eventually, years later, my dad also came to know Jesus. My parents stayed together for over fifty-five years and had a strong love.

So, if you think you're alone, you're not! Call on the name of Jesus. Have faith; trust the Lord with all your heart, and He will supply your needs. We can't make decisions or choices for other people, but we can make a bad situation a miracle in the hands of God!

Because of my home life, I thought I would never get married. I didn't trust men. I began praying for God to bring the man into my life that He would pick for me, if that was possible. One night, my older sister and her husband took me with them to a get-together at a friend's house. It was getting late and her husband didn't want to leave yet, so he asked their good friend, Ron, to take me home. Well, we left, and he asked me if I wanted to stop for some pie and coffee. I said, "Sure."

We stopped and talked for a very long time. He drove me home, and we kissed. As I went into my house, he said, "I'm going to marry you someday, Toni!" *Wow, I thought, what a jerk; he thinks I am so gullible!* I also knew that he was dating someone at that time. Well, there were my trust issues! "Men are all alike!" As time went on, I would see Ron around, as he was my sister and her husband's friend. We were cordial, but that was all. About two years later, Ron asked me out. I was apprehensive but said yes. He was so cute, with big, sky-blue eyes. We went to dinner and he was very easy to talk to. After that we both dated other people, but occasionally we would go out. One night I was going to a youth Bible study. Ron's sister was the leader, as their family went to our church. Ron was there, and he completely dedicated his life to Jesus that night. Not long after that we started dating, exclusive of anyone else. He asked me to marry him, and I said yes! God knew all the time who would be my husband. When God does something, He does it right! For thirty-eight years Ron was my best friend, my true love, my confidant, so much more than I imagined.

I had so many insecurities and trust issues because of my upbringing. Ron always knew what to say, and challenged me to be a better and stronger person. I called him my rock.

Ron and I have four children, and as they were born I would always pray for them to grow up to love God with all their hearts, and that God would keep them and guide them in His will and protection, and that the spouse God had for each of them would be protected and led by the Lord. I can truly say that God is faithful. Each of my daughters married amazing husbands who love the Lord with all their hearts and love their wives and children more than themselves—and even love their mother-in-law. My son is not married yet, but I know without a doubt that she's someone special and coming soon.

I now pray for my grandchildren and great-grandchildren, for their future—to love the Lord and live a blessed and fulfilled life of purpose.

God works in mysterious ways, His wonders to perform!

REFLECTION: GOD KNOWS

The good news for us is that God knows us! The Bible tells us that He knew us before we were in the womb; He formed us and He knows everything we have done—and even the things we have not even thought of yet.

Jeremiah 1:5 (KJV) "Before I formed thee in the belly I knew thee; and before thou camest forth out of the womb I sanctified thee."

Our childhood upbringing is so significant to the way we think and behave as we get older. Even as adults we are struggling with things from our past. Memories seem to attach themselves to us, the way we think, and even the way we act and react. But I want you to know that you can be victorious over these issues! God is the answer. He knows us better than we know ourselves. If you have chosen to serve God, His promises for you are "Yes" and "Amen"!

Jeremiah 29:11 (KJV) "For I know the thoughts that I think toward you, saith the Lord, thoughts of peace, and not of evil, to give you an expected end."

2 Peter 1:2-4 (KJV) "Grace and peace be multiplied unto you through the knowledge of God, and of Jesus our Lord, according as his divine power hath given unto us all things that pertain unto life and godliness, through the knowledge of him that hath called us to glory and virtue: whereby are given unto us exceeding great and precious promises: that by these ye might be partakers of the divine nature, having escaped the corruption that is in the world through lust."

Continue to read 2 Peter 1:5-11.

Silence is Golden

Sometimes we get into circumstances where we feel that we need to verbally defend ourselves, or even justify ourselves to others. The Bible says to be at peace with all men and to bless those that persecute you. One day my granddaughter Ellie went on social media—Facebook. It was just after the presidential election of 2016. President Trump was elected, and there were people who were upset and looting and rioting. Ellie got on and said, "Instead of rioting, why don't we see what this man has to say, and what he plans on doing?" Immediately, she got a horrible and angry response, full of profanity. When my daughter and I read it, I thought Ellie would respond. I was shocked that someone would react so viciously. It was an intense reaction to such a simple statement.

Instead of responding, Ellie was silent. In a few minutes, others got on and defended Ellie. I was impressed and so proud that Ellie did not get pulled into a verbal battle. If we hold our tongues, it stops the fire. It's hard to argue with an opponent who is silent. I talked to Ellie later and told her how proud I was of her. It turned out that the other person who gave the outburst was actually a distant relative, and would definitely be at family functions in the future. The fact that Ellie refrained from responding is a testament to the Lord. I asked why she didn't say anything, and she said, "I knew it was useless, and really a waste of time." She holds no grudge and is really fine about the whole thing. Sometimes being the light means keeping silent. Let God fight our battles. It was so amazing to me that another person spoke up for Ellie. The whole circumstance made the angry person look trivial. Be careful not to be pulled into situations just by being quick to react, losing your peace of mind, and allowing drama in your life. God's Word says, "Vengeance is mine... saith the Lord" (Romans 12:19 KJV). Satan roams about seeking whom he may devour. But when we stay cool, grounded in God, that stops him in his tracks. It's like putting out a fire!

The tongue is a tiny organ, but it can cause a lot of turmoil. Remember, our words are containers of blessings or curses. We can make a person's day great by just using a few nice words. Or we can hurt and cause despair with negative words. Romans 8:9-10 tells us that if we are in the Spirit, God dwells in us. And if Christ is in you, the body is dead, but the mind of the Spirit is life and peace. We need to break the habit of negative words and speak what God thinks of us, not what the world says. God sees our potential. Stop telling yourself, "I can't do anything! I'm so stupid!" Don't let Satan take you down that road. Speak words of truth: "I am the head and not the tail! I can do all things through Christ who strengthens me!" We must decide to believe God's Word and what He says about ourselves. Live life to its fullest. Set your mind on the Word of God, and the tongue will follow.

My second daughter Regina, when she was in college, had a group of friends she felt close to. She was always going out of her way to be there for them when they needed her. As it turned out, she found out they were talking about her behind her back and lying about situations in their lives. She felt betrayed, and it really hurt her. She decided to not get dragged into the drama by telling others what they did or gossiping about the situation. She decided to pray for them. God not only healed her heart but caused some real healing in their lives too. They later told her they were sorry and really missed her in their lives. God is just and faithful to take care of us if we serve and trust Him.

My youngest daughter Alyssa had a similar situation. Her best friend of many years, who went on numerous family vacations with us and really felt like part of the family, turned a complete 180 and became a whole different person after high school. Alyssa thought she knew her so well. It's hard to lose someone you have shared so much of your life with. We will never understand these kinds of situations in our lives. Alyssa and her friend still talk on occasion, but the friendship will never be the same. Life has a way of changing course when we least expect it.

Sometimes in our lives there are circumstances that are out of our control. Betrayal from people we love and care about, dishonesty in people we've trusted. It can be very disheartening. It can bring us down so low that we think we'll never recover. There really is no escape from life's heartaches and troubles, but when we live with faith, we can overcome it. The Word of God says, "I will never leave you nor forsake you" (Hebrews 13:5 ESV). We are really never alone, even in our darkest moments. Jesus is always there to comfort and heal our broken hearts. Because of faith, we can grieve our losses and still keep our joy.

REFLECTION:
SILENCE IS GOLDEN

The Bible talks a lot about the power of our words. We all know from life experience that harsh words can start a fight, and that calm words can heal a heart.

James 3:10 (KJV) "Out of the same mouth proceedeth blessing and cursing. My brethren, these things ought not so to be."

The taming of the tongue only comes from the Holy Spirit. We must renew our minds every day by reading the Word of God to fill our hearts with His grace and truth in His love. Choose to speak words that edify each other, instead of words of anger and hurt.

"A slip of the foot you may soon recover, but a slip of the tongue you may never get over." – Benjamin Franklin

Proverbs 15:1 (KJV) "A soft answer turneth away wrath: but grievous words stir up anger."

Proverbs 18:21 (KJV) "Death and life are in the power of the tongue: and they that love it shall eat the fruit thereof."

The Bible tells us that there will be a day of judgment, and every idle word will be judged! God is very serious about the way we talk to each other.

Matthew 12:36 (KJV) "But I say unto you, that every idle word that men shall speak, they shall give account thereof in the day of judgement. For... by thy words thou shalt be condemned."

Sometimes when we have been verbally attacked by others, we want to strike back with words of accusation, or name calling—something hurtful. The Lord tells us in His Word to let Him fight back for us. In Psalm 23:5 (KJV) it tells us: "Thou preparest a table before me in the presence of mine enemies." When we let God fight for us, we are vindicated in the presence of those that spitefully hurt us.

Romans 12:19 (KJV) "Dearly beloved, avenge not yourselves, but rather give place unto wrath: for it is written, Vengeance is mine; I will repay, saith the Lord."

James 1:19 (KJV) "Wherefore, my beloved brethren, let every man be swift to hear, slow to speak, slow to wrath."

Discipline

Discipline is a virtue that affects the rest of your life, from being on time to your job, to saying "no" when "yes" would be more fun. It means not just reacting to life events, but having goals to accomplish a purpose. So much that needs to be learned comes from discipline.

The definition of *discipline* is: a system of rules governing conduct; training that corrects, molds, or perfects the mental faculties or moral character; self-control; punishment.

Discipline is so important in our lives! Without it, we have no borders or boundaries. Integrity is being a person who does the right thing even when no one is looking. Without discipline there is no self-control. Joy is diminished; we become self-involved and selfish, lacking respect for ourselves and others.

As parents, the Bible instructs us in Proverbs 22:6 to train up a child in the way he should go, and when he is old, he will not depart from it. When I was eleven years old, I gave my heart to the Lord, and even at that early age the Lord gave me a deep desire to know the Bible. I read it many times, and the Lord instilled in me the importance of learning His Word. When we had our first child, Annette, I got a children's Bible and began reading a story every day. This continued with my other children until they were grown. So, now the tradition lives on, and they read the Bible with their children also. It's a foundation they will carry and know all of their lives.

The foundation of knowing who God is and what His Word says is what brings us to repentance. Repentance leads us to a willing heart, ready to receive instruction. Each of us is so different and unique. If you have several children, you may have to use several different means of training or discipline. In Ecclesiastes it warns us not to provoke our children while we train or teach them.

An example would be: with one of my daughters, if you spoke loudly or angrily, she would cry and be sorry immediately. Another daughter was not bothered at all by words, but needed a little more action to bring the right attitude and to change the behavior. That is where the training comes in, "in the way they should go." Know your children, and listen to them so you don't cause anger, but instead, repentance and forgiveness.

When training your children, be clear as to what you expect. Whenever we would go to a restaurant or to a friend's house, or even to the grocery store, I would tell my children how I expected them to act—and if that didn't happen, what the consequence would be when we got home. Always say what you mean and mean what you say! They are always watching you to see if you will keep your word. I love to give praise where it is due. So, when they did what I expected I would tell them how proud I was of them. Sometimes a treat was in order.

The last definition of *discipline* is punishment. It's definitely a consequence of poor choices in life. As a child growing up, discipline in my home was usually done in anger; it sometimes caused fear, other times resentment and anger.

When I became a parent, I really prayed for direction in all aspects of raising my children. One big one for me was how to discipline in love. One way that God showed me was to never discipline in anger. The Bible says to be angry and sin not. We can be angry without letting the anger control our actions. So, when my children were rebellious or disobedient, I would have them go to their room for a cool-off time. I would tell them what they did wrong and have them tell me back what they did. I always explained why they would have a consequence coming and what it would be. I would administer the consequence, and have them stay in their room until they could change their attitude and come out and apologize. We always hugged, and I always said "I love you" to my children. The whole point of discipline is to help bring remorse and repentance with a good heart, always bringing understanding of why punishment was needed. Never hold a grudge with your children; when it's over, it's over. Be careful of the words you use: "You're so stupid!" "You never listen!" "You're a brat!" "Idiot!" These kinds of words only cause hurt and disgrace. It makes your children feel like a disappointment to you, never feeling good enough. This lasts a lifetime. So again, we see the power of our words! Don't be weary in well doing; as you are consistent, you will see results.

Different forms of discipline could be:

1. Being on restriction, staying home from coveted events, or in their room for a reasonable period of time.
2. No social media, iPhone, iPad, computer, or even television.
3. Sometimes just a good, serious talk is all it takes; letting them know that you expect more of them, as you know they are capable of better behavior.

For smaller children:

1. Time out, usually one minute for each year of age. Four years old=four minutes. Re-administer if behavior doesn't change.
2. Spanking—only on the buttocks. Usually only if rebellious or using dangerous behavior.

Whatever form of discipline you use, be sure that as parents, you agree. If they see you argue over this, it causes them to be confused and angry about the outcome. United you stand; divided you fall.

When you are disciplining your children, make sure they know that you mean business. Have them look into your eyes, so they understand what you're saying. Use your deep Mama or Daddy voice if you need to get their attention—it really works.

Try to live your life as an example to your children. When we do the right thing but have a bad attitude, we lose the blessing. We must expect great things from our God. He sees us and knows us better than anyone. Our troubles become stepping-stones when we trust God. No one can keep you from your destiny—just you. Change your mind, look at the positive in life, and trust God even when you don't understand the situation around you or why things are going in this direction. Remember, God is the potter; we are the clay. The spinning process is the molding; we are becoming something beautiful and useful in its perfect purpose.

Remember Joshua and the battle of Jericho:

In Joshua 6, God said to Joshua to have the people march around the walls of Jericho once for six days in silence, and on the seventh day to march seven times in silence, then blow the trumpets and shout, "for the Lord has given you this city" (verse 16).

The walls fell flat! God had a strategy to cause fear in the hearts of the people in the city, and in the chaos, it was overtaken. Be faithful to what God tells you, and He will do the rest. He knows the beginning from the end. An ordinary day becomes an extraordinary day because of faithfulness. Our faithfulness in everyday life is a test of what we are made of. I believe that the Lord asked Joshua and the people to be silent so they would not murmur and complain to each other. Check yourself—no complaining or murmuring. If we are consistent and have a good attitude, this is a light to others, even our children. When we are faithful, God will trust us with more. It will bring favor from others because they see your integrity, and promotion will follow. This is the day the Lord has made. I will rejoice and be glad in it. Stay in faith and be patient. God is our Provider, and He brings promotion. In Ephesians 6 it tells us to put on the whole armor of God: 1.) The helmet of salvation; know who God is by reading His Word and keeping it in your heart and mind. 2.) The breastplate of righteousness; do the right thing and speak well of others. 3.) The shield of faith; quenching the fiery darts that come against us. Don't take offense easily from hurtful words or deeds. 4.) The belt of truth; be honest and trustworthy. 5.) Keep your feet in peace; don't be a gossip or troublemaker, getting people stirred up. 6.) The sword of the Spirit; know what God's Word says. The sword is the Word of God! It is stronger than any two-edged sword, cutting to the bone and even to the marrow (Hebrews 4:12)! If we purposefully get up each day and put on the armor of God, what a difference we would make in others' lives. Be the light, the salt, and the standard that God has called us to be.

When my son Richie was about twelve or thirteen years old, he had a time of not being his usual self—he was down in the dumps, looking at life through a dark light. He was unhappy and did not really know why. Sometimes life is just hard, and middle school is definitely a trying time in a child's life. There are lots of changes physically and socially, and the expectations and pressures of life become a little more serious. I noticed his attitude change and asked him what was wrong; he said, "Nothing, everything is fine." So, I decided one night to go into his room and just talk and visit about things going on in my day, and frustrations I was dealing with. He began to open up and share some of the pressures he was feeling, and how some of his friends were changing. We talked for a long time, and I said, "Let's pray about it and give our worries and fears to Jesus." He said yes, and we prayed together. I felt it was a special time together; I was so blessed. His attitude was definitely lighter, and I could see my son maturing before my eyes. God is so good; He is the lifter of our soul, and He brings peace to our hearts even when we don't know what exactly to ask for. In Psalm 91:1 (NKJV) it says, "He who dwells in the secret place of the Most High shall abide under the shadow of the almighty! I will say of the Lord, 'He is my refuge and my fortress; my God, in Him will I trust!'" Another prayer I love is in Matthew 6:9-13 (KJV): the Lord's Prayer. "Our Father which art in heaven, Hallowed be thy name. Thy kingdom come, thy will be done in earth, as it is in heaven. Give us this day our daily bread. And forgive us our debts, as we forgive our debtors. And lead us not into temptation, but deliver us from evil: For thine is the kingdom, and the power, and the glory, forever. Amen." Sometimes in life, we feel we should be forgiven for things we've said or done to others. Maybe we think our situation is different—we did not intend to cause bad feelings, but it still happened. Yet when someone else says something offensive or does something to us that we don't like, we are quick to be angry or to judge and hold grudges. But this prayer says that we are forgiven our sins as we forgive others. Be careful not to presume others' intentions and faults and to give yourself the benefit of the doubt. We all sin and fall short of the glory of God. Forgiveness is essential to having a blessed and fulfilled life. Because we are forgiven much, we must forgive others!

Because of God's grace and mercy to us, we must keep believing in the love and faithfulness of God. Then anxiety and fear and worry and strife will leave, in Jesus' name!

REFLECTION: DISCIPLINE

Without discipline in our lives, the consequences can be devastating. Cheating and lying, being a slacker for our own satisfaction—it usually leads to one looking out for themselves, alone. It causes others to think of you as untrustworthy.

Honesty and loyalty are attributes of discipline that one may not think of. The rewards of self-discipline bring honor and respect to you and your whole family.

A truthful man or women is a treasure in today's world. Our word used to be a bond, but now the lack of integrity is far and wide.

Proverbs 16:3 (KJV) "Commit thy works unto the Lord, and thy thoughts shall be established."

Proverbs 23:12 (KJV) "Apply thine heart unto instruction, and thine ears to the words of knowledge."

God wants us to be the standard; He wants us to be the people He can trust to obey His direction, keep His commandments, and be trustworthy so that He can use us in mighty ways. Financially giving to what He asks us to give to, serving where He wants us to serve, and living our lives in God's purpose with dedication, so that our children have a strong legacy of wisdom in God's Word.

Deuteronomy 6:5-9 (KJV) "And thou shalt love the Lord thy God with all thine heart, and with all thy soul, and with all thy might. And these words, which I command thee this day, shall be in thine heart: And thou shalt teach them diligently unto thy children, and shalt talk of them when thou sittest in thine house, and when thou walkest by the way, and when thou liest down, and when thou risest up. And thou shalt bind them for a sign upon thine hand, and they shall be as frontlets between thine eyes. And thou shalt write them upon the posts of thy house, and on thy gates."

Emotions

Life may not change as quickly as we would like, but we can change how we respond to life.

Emotion: a state of strong feeling; a conscious mental reaction accompanied by behavioral changes in the body.

Emotions change all the time. Love, joy, anger, hate, fear, guilt, and jealousy. Living life or being led by our emotions is like a roller coaster that doesn't stop—a frustrating life. Choose and decide to not let your feelings dictate your day or even your life. You are valuable to everyone around you. You are an influence and a force in your family's lives. Make it be a positive influence. Go to God; He is able to help you change the pattern of trusting your emotions instead of living life to its fullest.

When I was a little girl, my mother used a pressure cooker in the kitchen for cooking. It scared me, because it always looked like it was about to explode at any minute. Sometimes our emotions get the best of us, and we resemble a pressure cooker ready to go off when things don't go our way. If you are overcome with negative emotions, stop and say the name of Jesus—say it over and over: "Jesus, Jesus." There is power in His name. Ask Him for clear thinking and peace and guidance. He is always faithful to answer those who call His name.

My husband and I had been married for about twenty years. We owned a trucking company in Fontana, California, and were doing quite well. We had our four children, a beautiful home, a pool, and an SUV in the driveway; everything was going great! We were offered a huge contract for our trucking business. It was to haul pipe up to the Mojave Desert for what was to be the largest pipeline in the state at that time. We looked at the numbers and thought that this would be a great way to bring us to the next level of business. We knew that this was a union job, so we had to join a labor union and a workers' union. It was an expensive endeavor, but we knew that the profit would come at the completion of the job, which would take about six months. We were all in. Our fuel source extended our credit line. Our tire and parts source trusted us, as we always paid our bills. It was a long job, but everything went ahead, moving along pretty smoothly. We finally finished the job and were waiting for our final payment. This is where we would pay off our creditors and finally see the profit.

The company said that payment would be here in two weeks. It never came; phone calls said two more weeks. It never came, and then they stopped answering our calls. By now everyone needed their money. We were sinking fast. We couldn't pay our bills. This company was well-known, established in Chicago. They had lots of businesses and airplanes. Money was not an issue for them, but they decided that we were a small business and they just didn't pay us. We talked to lawyers, and they said because we had no money to pay up front it wasn't worth the fight, as our opponent was too big. Legal fees would eat up all the profit. We felt like we had let everyone down. We tried to sell equipment, but by the time we realized we weren't getting paid, creditors were at our door repossessing equipment. We lost our business and eventually our home. It was a scary time. It was not our fault! We had done everything right! It was not fair! We found a house to rent not too far away so our children could stay in their same schools. It wasn't a bad house, but the décor was stuck in the 70s: orange tile floors, shag carpet, and blue wallpaper in the kitchen. I became a little bitter. Why was this happening? We always worked hard and were honest people. My husband hated letting people down—and especially his family. He was working hard to make some money to get us out of this hole. He never complained, but was withdrawn. It was really hard on him. I knew it was just stuff, just a house, just a vehicle. But we had worked so hard to get here. It was a huge loss. My emotions were all over the place. I was angry—not at anyone in particular, just not happy. I shed a lot of tears. I was trying to deal with it all; there were good days and bad. Creditors were calling all the time, and our credit was gone. My husband started a new business—a roofing company—and things started getting better. I got a job selling clothes at a boutique in Newport Beach. It took me almost a year to get back to myself. Bitterness and "why me" are thieves to a happy life. I was so sorry that I wasted that year being upset and unhappy. I know it affected my family, and I was ashamed. I don't ever want to live life like that again. I refused to let bitterness take hold of my life any longer. I painted every room in that house myself, and took down that blue wallpaper and the 70s drapes. My husband put up ceiling fans, and it was home. When things get hard or out of my control, I immediately go to God and ask for help, and He's always there. You don't have to look very far to see someone worse off than you. So, count your blessings every day! It took us twelve years to save enough money to buy another house. We moved to Texas for a change. Life is good, and my family is very strong! My husband's inner strength to work hard, keep going, and be positive has taught me and my children that we can do all things through Christ who strengthens us. Renew your mind every day; read the Word of God and believe it. It is food for our soul and health to our mind and body. Cast your cares on Jesus, because He cares for you. When we pray, we get what we need to endure life's trials with a good attitude. We can't always change our circumstances, but with God we can change what we do and how we act.

Fear: a distressing emotion aroused by impending danger, evil, pain, etc., whether the threat is real or imagined. Feeling of dread, terror, panic, dismay, and apprehension.

Early on in our marriage, about our third year, my husband and his brothers owned a boat and barge company in Alaska. They would buy boats in San Diego, California, and take them to San Pedro to work on. Then they would sail the boats up to Prudhoe Bay, Alaska, to work on the pipeline, hauling equipment and crews. This time he would have to be gone at least three months. We thought that in the long run, the financial benefit was worth it. We had just bought a house, and our little girl Annette was two years old. Things were good. After my husband was gone awhile, I heard on the news about a serial killer in our county and area. He would come in windows into homes and rape and kill. I began to become very fearful. I wouldn't be out after dark, always making sure to come home early to lock up the house and feel safe. I began getting weird phone calls, with heavy breathing and profanities. I suspected a man at the grocery store but couldn't be sure. We had a doggy door off the kitchen porch door, and one day when I came home, things in my house were turned upside down and quite a mess. Nothing was taken that I noticed. My brother-in-law came over and said it looked like someone had come in through the doggy door. There was no break-in and no windows were disturbed. So he boarded the doggy door closed. But of course I was even more fearful, not knowing who it might be. I never slept at night. I watched TV, usually Trinity Broadcasting Network (a Christian station), until the TV would shut off at midnight. Then I would sit up with a gun the rest of the night, just in case someone tried to get in. This house had a hallway that went back to the bedrooms, and as I prayed for safety I would see a glimpse of angels' gowns walking up and down that hallway. I know that God was trying to comfort me, but I just couldn't let go of the fear. One day I went to the beach with my little girl. I stayed a little late, and traffic was bad so I got home later than usual. I rushed into the house and got Annette settled and made sure the house was locked up. I went to make

dinner. It was now dark, and someone rang my door-
bell. I looked out the side window shutters and saw a
man with long hair and jeans. I had never seen him before. I went to the door (closed) and said, "Can I help
you?" He said, "Oh, I just wanted to tell you that your
headlights on your car are left on, and I don't want your
battery to die." I pretended that my husband was home,
yelling, "Honey, we left the headlights on in the car." I
told the man thank you, then I went to the shutters to
watch him leave. He was gone! I couldn't see him on the
porch or walking away; he was just gone. I knew that I
had to go outside and turn off the headlights. I called
my mom and told her what happened and asked her to
hold on the phone while I went to turn off lights, and if
I wasn't back in a few minutes to call the police. I ran
out to shut off lights and locked the car, and there was
my mom pulling up. I later felt like God sent that man
or maybe an angel to my door so my car would not be
dead in the morning. Hebrews 13:2 (KJV), "Be not for-
getful to be hospitable: for thereby some have enter-
tained angels unawares." My mom stayed for dinner,
and we sat on the living room floor praying. She knew
I was afraid, so we prayed for victory over fear! It had
to be maybe two hours of talking, crying, and praying,
when a bright light came through the windows directly
on us! We felt the warmth of God and peace come over

both of us. It was like a heaviness was lifted from me. No more life of fear. I was delivered! I realized how my fear was absolutely nothing. It's the feeling of anticipation of what terrible thing might happen or what might come. Actually, it's like a façade, based on what we believe might happen. Faith and fear are opposites. Faith is confidence and trust in God, knowing that He knows what is ahead of us and will protect us either from it or through it. We walk by faith, not sight. Fear is Satan's way of gripping us and binding us to keep us from living a victorious life. Thank you, Jesus, for your power, love, and faith! My mother has always been a faithful and committed prayer partner with unending faith. If anyone in our family needs prayer, we all call Grandma!

If you have asked Jesus Christ to be your Savior and Lord and have repented of your sins, then you are a child of God and entitled to every promise in the Bible, because you have the Holy Spirit living inside you. Read God's Word and your faith will grow, and you will be equipped to live a better life. Don't be regretful. No matter what has happened in your past, or what you've done, when you ask Jesus into your heart then you are already forgiven! In Romans 8:1 (KJV) it says, "There is now no condemnation to those who are in Christ Jesus." We must come like a little child and believe, living in truth and love and forgiveness and purpose! Choose Fun!

REFLECTION: EMOTIONS

The way we connect a thought to an emotion is how we will relate to it. Such as the thought: I'm at home alone. This is true. I can think of it as sad because there is no one with me, or happy because I can make popcorn and watch whatever I want to. I can be angry because my family has not asked me to come over, or fearful because I am alone and someone could break in. Wow, Satan has a lot of options to play with to cause us to have an emotion that could be really gripping and scary. If we know what God's Word says, then we can look at our circumstances with confidence, knowing that we are all right.

Hebrews 13:5 (KJV) "I will never leave thee nor forsake thee."

We can take hold of our emotions and attitudes and choose to make a better choice of what to believe.

1. Being angry is really a waste of time; unless we talk things out with the person who caused the anger, we are really just being angry on our own.

2. Being fearful is Satan's special tool to keep us in the dark, not seeing the truth.
3. Isaiah 54:17 (KJV) "No weapon that is formed against thee shall prosper."
4. James 4:7 (KJV) "Submit yourselves therefore to God. Resist the devil, and he will flee from you."
5. Nehemiah 8:10 (KJV) "The joy of the Lord is your strength."

Be victorious in your walk with Christ, taking control of your emotions with the Word of God!

Suggested reading: Psalm 91:1-16.

Blessed

The Lord is good! His mercy endures forever. These are the words the Lord gave me at the age of eleven, when I was first introduced to the glory of God and the Holy Spirit. I went to a ladies' prayer meeting with my mother. There I received my gift of the Holy Spirit, and the interpretation was a verse that is well-known in the book of Psalms: "The Lord is Good, and his mercy endures forever!" I say it every morning—it has been part of my prayer life ever since.

I can honestly say that my life has been extremely blessed. My mother gave her heart to the Lord as a young woman, and because of that, our whole household was saved. Because of her dedication to the Lord, I sought out a man who loved God with all his heart. Together we raised our family to serve God—not just on Sundays, but every day—acknowledging that Jesus Christ is Lord and Savior, through the good times and the bad. Life goes by so quickly. My children are grown and have families of their own now. Each of my daughters have married men who serve and love God, put their families above everything else, work hard, and are a blessing to us all. My son serves God with all his heart and is a blessing to so many around him. I couldn't be prouder, or more thankful to the Lord for being true to His Word and proving that if we are willing to serve Him with our whole life, He is faithful and just to fulfill His promises. My family is a testimony of God's gracious and mighty Word. Today I have sixteen grandchildren and one on the way, and also three great-grandchildren. The legacy my mother gave us when she decided to serve God is growing, and I know that there is more to come. As for me and my house, we will serve the Lord!

It has been eleven years now since Ron, my husband, was taken to be with the Lord. In those years I had become pretty independent, working full time, running my home, planting my garden, and spending time at the Lord's house and with many outings and gatherings with my friends and family. They were years of joy and blessings and contentment. My life was full.

The Lord had something else in mind for me. One day I was at the airport, getting ready to get on a plane to go and visit my mom and sisters. I received a text from a man, Mike, whom I had just met at a Rough Riders game. He was my son-in-law's employer and was the man who had sponsored the Rough Riders event for all employees and family—it was awesome, and we all had a great time. The text said, "Would you mind if I call you sometime?" I was very shocked and replied, "I'm on my way to California, and I will be home in about a week."

I later found out that his daughter and son-in-law, who also worked with my son-in-law, had seen me at a birthday party for the kids. His daughter Jennifer had told her dad that he should meet me, because I seemed like a really nice lady. She also had a dream that Mike and I got married.

I was not interested in a relationship—had not even thought about it; my life was great. I'd had other men try to get to know me and it really was a waste of time. I just wasn't interested.

So, Mike called me after I got home, and we talked a little. With life so busy for both of us, we mostly texted. This went on for a few months. I was not ready to date, nor did I even think I would want to. My life was in order, everything was set; even my future was planned out. This would be a life-changing event that I wasn't sure I was willing to take. I was really praying about this, making sure that I was staying in God's will. My marriage with Ron was so good, the bar was set extremely high. I did not want to get into a relationship that would be less than that. One night I woke up, and the Lord spoke to me and clearly said, "I can do it again!" I began crying and asked God, "Why would you do that for me twice, when some don't get it once?" I felt His love cover me like a warm cover and felt a peace that was unexplainable. The love of God is amazing.

As we kept talking, Mike was so amazing. He loved God with all his heart and was winning me over. We shared about our lives, our families, and what we wanted for our futures. Months later, we started dating. God had big plans for us. We got engaged in April, 2019, and in July, 2019 we had a beautiful wedding. Mike also has a large family—five children, four daughters and one son. He has fourteen grandchildren. Our wedding had most all of the families there—it was a lot of fun, and a beautiful sight.

Mike and I will be married one year in July. It has been so wonderful. Life is different for me now, and God knew more about me than I do. We can trust God. His love for us is more than we can comprehend or even understand.

REFLECTION:
BLESSED

One thing I have learned through the years:
Don't put God in a box. There is nothing impossible with God. The Lord knows us so much better than we even know ourselves.

Luke 12:6-7 (KJV) "Are not five sparrows sold for two farthings, and not one of them is forgotten before God? But even the very hairs of your head are all numbered. Fear not therefore: ye are of more value than many sparrows."

Zephaniah 3:17 (KJV) "The Lord thy God in the midst of thee is mighty; he will save, he will rejoice over thee with joy; he will rest in his love, he will joy over thee with singing."

Romans 5:8 (KJV) "But God commendeth his love toward us, in that, while we were yet sinners, Christ died for us."

Ephesians 3:17-19 (KJV) "That Christ may dwell in your hearts by faith; that ye, being rooted and grounded in love, may be able to comprehend with all saints what is the breadth, and length, and depth, and height; and to know the Love of Christ, which passeth knowledge, that ye might be filled with all the fullness of God."

Accept Jesus Christ as your Lord and Savior, and you will never be alone!

Choose to serve God, and live life on purpose!

Choose Fun!

References

Jeremiah 29:11, NIV

Psalm 23, KJV

Acts 6:5, story of Stephen, Bible

Nehemiah 8:10,KJV

Proverbs 17:22, KJV

Philippians 4:13, KJV

Jeremiah 1:5, NIV

Romans 12:19, KJV

Definition of *discipline*: Merriam-Webster

Joshua 6, story of Joshua, Bible

Hebrews 4:12, KJV

Matthew 6:9, KJV

Definition of *emotions*: Merriam-Webster

Definition of *fear*: Dictionary.com

Hebrews 13:2, KJV

Hebrews1 13:5, KJV

Joshua 24:15, KJV

Romans 8:28, KJV

Romans 8:1, KJV

Romans 8:5, KJV

Proverbs 25:18, KJV

Proverbs 22:6, KJV

Proverbs 17:22, KJV

Proverbs 16:3, KJV

Proverbs 23:12, KJV

Proverbs 15:1, KJV

Proverbs 18:21, KJV

Proverbs 16:24, KJV

Psalms 91:1, NKJV

Psalms 106:3-5, KJV

Deuteronomy 6:5, KJV

James 3:10, KJV

James 4:14, KJV

James 4:7, KJV

Isaiah 57:17, KJV

Acts 6:5, KJV

Luke 12:6-7, KJV

Ephesians 6:12-17, KJV

Ephesians 3:17-19, KJV

Galatians 6:9, KJV

Galatians 5:22-23, KJV

Matthew 12:36-37, KJV

John 15:4-5, KJV

John 3:16, KJV

Ecclesiastes 3:1-4, KJV

Philippians 2:3-5, KJV

2 Peter 1:2-11, KJV

TONETA WITTE

About the Author

I came to know Jesus when I was eleven years old. I dedicated my life to Him, and to raising my children to honor the Lord, to loving my husband, and to pursuing God's purpose for my life every day! God is good!

Toni Witte

CPSIA information can be obtained
at www.ICGtesting.com
Printed in the USA
LVHW050935090920
665425LV00007B/8